108 QUIRKY FACTS FOR SUPER SMART KIDS

A Collection of Quirky Weird Facts about Space, Technology, Ancient History and much more...

by

ANDY RYAN

THIS BOOK
BELONGS TO

108 QUIRKY FACTS FOR SUPER SMART KIDS

A Collection of Quirky Facts about Space, Technology, Ancient History and Much More...

Andy Ryan

Paperback ISBN: 9798873871629

Copyright © 2024 – Andy Ryan

Disclaimer: This book on quirky facts for kids is intended to provide fun and educational information in an engaging format. While we have made every effort to ensure the accuracy and reliability of the facts presented herein, it is important to note that knowledge is constantly evolving, and new discoveries may have emerged since the publication of this book. Additionally, some topics may be sensitive or subject to cultural differences. Parents, guardians, and educators should review the content to ensure it aligns with their values and is appropriate for the age and maturity level of the child.

HOW TO USE THIS BOOK

- **Interest Alignment**: Skim through the book to identify facts that align with your child's interests. This ensures engagement and enthusiasm.

- **Interactive Learning**: Read the facts together with your child. Encourage them to ask questions and explore topics further. This promotes curiosity and a deeper understanding.

- **Daily Fact Routine**: Introduce a 'fact of the day' from the book. It's a fun way to incorporate learning into daily routines.

- **Link to School Subjects**: Relate the quirky facts to subjects your child is learning at school. This helps them see the real-world application of their schoolwork.

- **Encourage Research Skills**: If a fact sparks interest, help your child research more about it online or in other books. This enhances their research skills.

- **Discussion and Debate**: Discuss the facts with your child. Encourage them to form opinions or even challenge the facts, fostering critical thinking.

- **Creative Projects**: Use the facts as prompts for creative projects like drawing, writing stories, or conducting simple experiments.

- **Social Sharing**: Encourage your child to share these facts with friends or family. It's a great way for them to engage socially and practice communication skills.

- **Track Progress and Interests**: Note the facts that particularly interest your child. This can guide future educational and leisure activities.

- **Keep it Fun**: Remember, *most importantly*, the goal is to nurture a love for learning. Keep the atmosphere light and fun.

CONTENTS

INTRODUCTION

Welcome, young explorers, to '108 Quirky Facts for Super Smart Kids'. Reading a book about quirky facts is like opening a treasure chest of imagination.

Remember, learning is an ongoing adventure, and this book is just one step on your journey of discovery. You are encouraged to explore further, verify information, and stay curious about the world around you. The facts in this book are meant to serve as a starting point for young minds, fostering a love for learning and critical thinking. Always consult reliable sources and seek guidance from knowledgeable adults when in doubt.

To spur you on, each fact is followed by space for your additional notes or illustrations. So, feel free to explore, research, discover and note these down...

BIZARRE TRUTHS: WORLD OF UNUSUAL FOODS

Peanuts Aren't Nuts

Peanuts are legumes, not nuts. A legume is a type of plant that has seeds inside pods. Legumes include beans, lentils, and peas. True nuts, like almonds, walnuts, and chestnuts, grow on trees and do not have a pod that opens. Nuts are the seed of the fruit of these trees, and the fruit part is usually inedible. Peanuts grow underground. They start flowering above ground, but unlike tree nuts the peanut plant then develops its fruit, the peanut which matures underground.

The Banana-Strawberry Puzzle

In botanical terms, a berry is a simple fruit with seeds and pulp produced from the ovary of a single flower. It is also typically fleshy. Bananas fit this definition because they develop from a flower with one ovary and have a soft, fleshy middle. Therefore, scientifically, bananas are considered true berries. Strawberries, on the other hand, do not meet this botanical criterion. They are derived from a flower with multiple ovaries. What we think of as the fruit of a strawberry is a swollen part of the plant's stem called the receptacle. The tiny 'seeds' on the outside of a strawberry, commonly mistaken for seeds; they are technically individual fruits themselves.

China's Century Eggs

Century eggs, also known as thousand-year eggs, millennium eggs, or preserved eggs, are a traditional Chinese delicacy with a unique preparation method and distinctive taste. They have been a part of Chinese cuisine for centuries. The exact origin is unclear, but they are believed to have been discovered several hundred years ago in China. Despite their names, century eggs are not actually preserved for a century, a thousand years, or a millennium. The name is a reference to the egg's aged appearance and strong flavor. The preservation process takes several weeks to a few months. The preservation process transforms the eggs so that the yolk becomes a dark green or grey color with a creamy consistency, and the white turns into a dark brown, translucent jelly.

Poop Coffee

Civet coffee, or kopi Luwak, is one of the most distinctive and contentious coffees in the world. Unbelievably, it originates from poop! Coffee beans that have been consumed, broken down, and expelled by Asian palm civets are used to make the coffee. The beans are said to undergo fermentation during the civet's digestive process, which modifies the beans' flavor. The labor-intensive method of collecting the beans and the distinctive production process are the reasons behind Kopi Luwak's very high price. After being harvested, the beans are carefully cleaned and processed. High temperatures are used during the roasting process to ensure that the coffee is safe to consume.

Honey Never Spoils

As honey is mostly sugar, and it has very little water in it, it can stay good for a long, long time. As bacteria and germs, that spoil food, need water to live, they cannot survive in honey. Honey also has natural substances that act like preservatives such as acid and an ingredient that bees add called bee propolis, which helps to keep germs away.

Chocolate Record

In 2011 Thorntons in the UK set the record for producing the largest chocolate bar in terms of weight. It weighed 12,770lb (5,792kg), which is about the weight of an elephant. To make this gigantic chocolate bar, a lot of chocolate had to be melted and mixed. It required a huge space, big machines, and lots of people working together.

Orange Carrots

Carrots were not originally orange. Wild carrots are thought to have been purple or white with a thin, forked root. The orange carrot that is most common today is the result of selective breeding, which began in the 16th or 17th century in Central Europe. This breeding aimed to improve the vegetable's size, texture, and color, leading to the orange variety we are familiar with today. The purple, red, white, and yellow carrots still exist but are less common. Today, you can find carrots in a rainbow of colors, including the traditional orange as well as purple, red, yellow, and even black. These different colors come from different pigments, each with its own set of nutritional benefits.

Square Watermelons

Square watermelons were first developed in Japan. They were created to make them easier to stack and store in refrigerators, which are often smaller in Japan compared to those in Western countries. To grow a square watermelon, the fruit is placed inside a square, tempered glass case while it's still growing on the vine. As the watermelon grows, it takes the shape of the case. Because of their novelty and the labor involved in growing them, square watermelons are typically much more expensive than regular watermelons. They are often given as gifts or used as decorative items in Japan.

Chocolate as Currency

The use of chocolate as currency dates back to the ancient civilizations of Mesoamerica, including the Aztec and Maya cultures. These civilizations highly valued cacao beans, from which chocolate is made. Cacao beans were used as a form of currency by these civilizations. They were traded for goods and services, much like money is used today. This system was well established by the time the Spanish arrived in the New World.

Durian Fruit

In Southeast Asia, durian fruit is frequently referred to as the King of Fruits. Durian is highly valued as a delicacy and frequently used in ceremonies and special occasions in many Southeast Asian cultures. It is well known for having an overpowering scent that has been likened to raw sewage, turpentine, and rotting onions. In Southeast Asia, the smell is so strong that it is prohibited in a lot of hotels and public transportation. Many people adore the taste of durian, despite its strong odor. According to descriptions, the flavor is creamy and sweet, resembling a rich almond or vanilla custard combined with garlic.

Ice Cream

The history of ice cream begins thousands of years ago. Records date back to 200 BCE, when the Chinese were producing a dessert resembling frozen milk. Various cultures, including Chinese, Arab, Italian, French, and American, have influenced the development of ice cream throughout its history. Ice cream became more widely available when insulated ice houses were created in the 17th and 18th centuries, and the hand-cranked freezer was created in the 19th century. Ice cream was produced in large quantities and became widely accessible due to the industrial revolution and the development of mechanical refrigeration in the late 19th and early 20th centuries. With countless flavors and variations, ice cream has become a global dessert today, influenced by regional culinary traditions and tastes.

MYSTERIES OF THE ANCIENT PAST

Sphinx Riddles

The concept of the Sphinx testing people's wits is primarily rooted in Greek mythology. The Sphinx, a mythical creature, has the head of a human and the body of a lion. An ancient myth has it that it sat in the desert challenging travelers to solve its mind-bending puzzles. The Sphinx loved to test people's wits. Travelers had to answer the Sphinx's riddles to pass safely. The consequence of failure for those who could not answer the Sphinx's riddle was death and being eaten by the Sphinx.

Ancient Egyptian Mourning Rituals for Cats

One of the main reasons Ancient Egyptians shaved their eyebrows was as a sign of mourning, particularly when a family cat died. Cats were highly revered in Egyptian society, often associated with the goddess Bastet, who was the deity of home, fertility, and childbirth, as well as protector against evil spirits. It is said that when a family cat passed away, all members of the household would shave off their eyebrows as a sign of deep mourning and respect. The eyebrows would not be allowed to grow back until after the mourning period was complete, which could last several months.

Ming Dynasty Kite Messages

Kites were used for military communication during the Ming Dynasty. The kites served as a means to send messages over long distances, especially during sieges or when traditional communication methods were not possible. The design of the kites, including the shape and the patterns on them, could be used to relay strategic information, warnings, or other important messages to troops or allies. They were also used for surveillance. By flying a kite over enemy lines or territories, military leaders could gather information about enemy positions and movements, illustrating the ingenuity and resourcefulness in ancient Chinese military strategy.

Roman Fish Sauce Ice Cream

Romans had a strange taste for a sauce made from fermented fish called garum. They put it on almost everything, even desserts. It's like having fish-flavored ice cream. They had special buildings called ice houses to store ice, ready to be turned into the strangest desserts the ancient world had ever seen. Romans enjoyed their ice treats especially during events in the Colosseum. The Romans were the innovators of strange and surprising flavors.

Roman Baths

Roman baths were like fancy water parks made of marble. They were shiny, smooth, and very elegant. The Romans built caldariums with a hot plunge pool and frigidariums, where they could take a chilly plunge. Bath time was a serious affair, and Romans had helpers called slaves who would rub scented oils on their skin. Romans did not just take a quick dip, as their bath time could last for hours.

Togas

Togas were garments worn by Roman men, during the ancient Roman era. It was a long-draped garment made from a single piece of fabric. And worn to symbolize Roman citizenship. Slaves, foreigners, and women were not permitted to wear togas. The toga was seen as a symbol of peace as Roman men would wear the sagum, a type of military cloak, during wartimes.

Roman Roads

Romans built super straight roads. The saying 'All roads lead to Rome' was not just a saying, it was a fact. Romans built roads that connected their empire like a giant web. They used layers of rock, gravel, and sand to make sure their roads could withstand chariot races and marching soldiers. Romans even built bridges and tunnels to keep the ride going smoothly.

Mysterious Castle Moats

Castles were like super-fortresses, and they were surrounded by water-filled moats, mainly to keep enemies away. Moats were filled with fish, ducks, swans, and other water-loving creatures. To get into the castle, you needed to cross a drawbridge over the moat. Some moats had secret tunnels underneath the water. Castles with moats often had drawbridges. These were like special doors made of wood that could be lowered over the moat to let friends in and raised to keep enemies out.

Royal Falconry

Falconry is the art of training birds of prey, like falcons, to hunt. It has been around for thousands of years and was especially popular with kings and queens, which is why it is sometimes referred to as royal falconry. Falcons were not just pets; they were hunting friends. With razor-sharp talons, they could catch prey in the blink of an eye. Kings and queens even dressed their falcons in stylish little hoods. Their eyesight was so sharp that they could spot their prey from way up in the sky. Falcons were not just skilled hunters; they were also fast mail deliverers. Kings and queens used them to send messages over long distances. Falcons were incredible flyers, performing acrobatic stunts mid-air. Although it is called falconry, it is not just falcons that were used; hawks, eagles, and even owls were trained in falconry. Each type of bird has its unique hunting style and requires different training techniques.

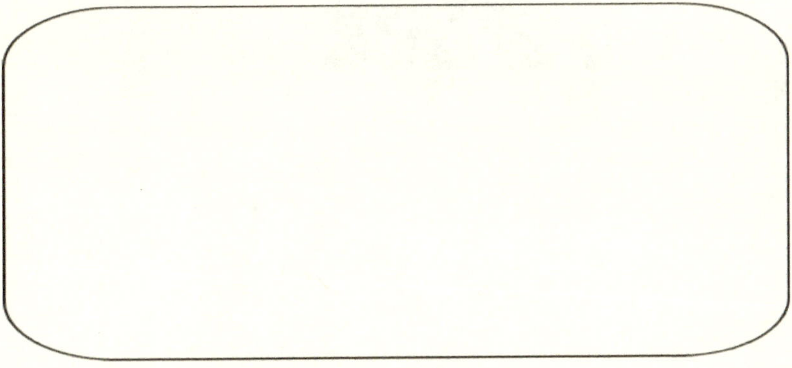

THE WEIRD & WONDROUS HUMAN BODY

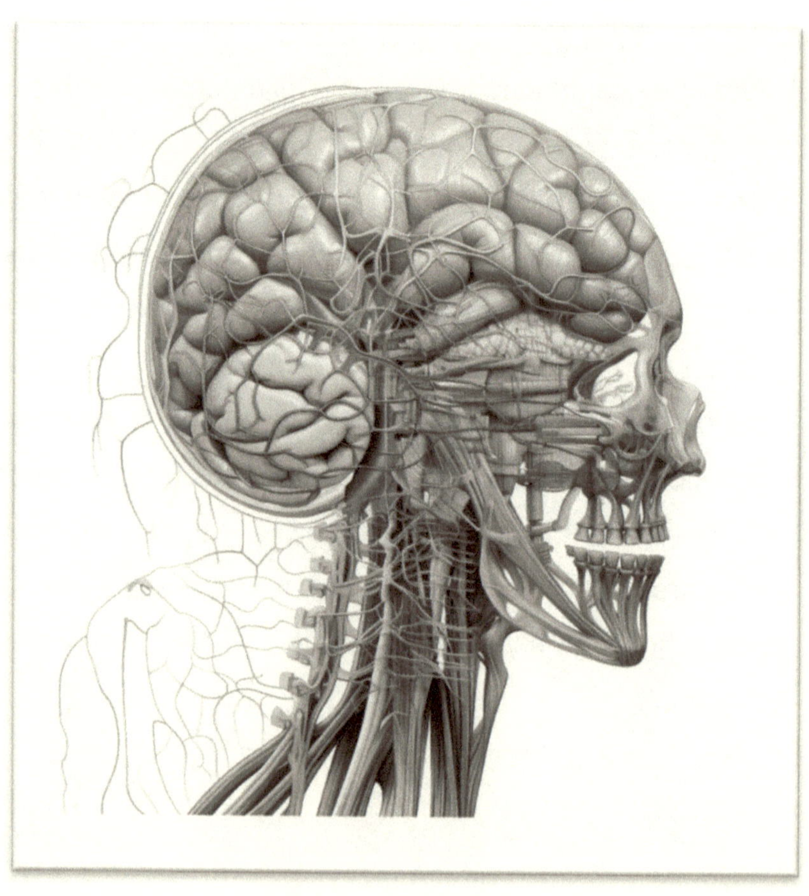

The Human Tongue

The claim that the tongue is the strongest muscle in the body is a common misconception, but it highlights the unique and impressive capabilities of the tongue. It is not a single muscle but a group of muscles that work together in a highly coordinated manner. This muscular organ is unique in that it is not attached to bones at both ends like skeletal muscles. It consists of a mix of intrinsic and extrinsic muscles. Intrinsic muscles allow the tongue to change its shape, such as rolling or elongating, while extrinsic muscles change its position extending it out of the mouth or moving it from side to side. This combination of muscles provides exceptional flexibility and range of motion.

The Power of Stomach Acid

Human stomach acid is believed to be extremely acidic, usually measuring between a pH of 1 and 2 when food is present. This acidity is strong enough to dissolve metal and is similar to battery acid. The high acidity is necessary to break down food into smaller, easier-to-digest components, especially proteins. Additionally, it aids in the destruction of dangerous bacteria and other pathogens that could be consumed along with food, offering a crucial line of defense against diseases. Stomach acid is highly corrosive, but it does not damage the stomach lining. This is due to the production of a thick, protective mucus by the stomach lining cells. This mucus creates a barrier to stop the stomach's tissue from being harmed by the acid. Furthermore, the stomach lining has a rapid rate of cell turnover, which means that before the acid can really harm the cells, they are swiftly replaced.

Human Bone Count

Humans have about 270 bones at birth, but only about 206 bones by the time they reach adulthood. Ossification, the process by which individual bones progressively fuse together over time, is the cause of this decrease in bone count. The merging of the bones in the spine and skull is a prime illustration of this. The skull's bones are not entirely fused in newborns and early children, allowing the brain to expand. These bones fuse together when a person ages, lowering their overall bone count.

Human Brain

Scientists have discovered that the human brain is more active while we are asleep than when we are watching TV. Contrary to what many might think, the brain is highly active during sleep. Prolonged TV watching, especially of non-stimulating content, can lead to lower brain activity in regions involved in cognitive and emotional processes. It may also contribute to a more passive mindset, reducing the tendency to actively engage in more stimulating intellectual activities. Sleep plays a crucial role in neural plasticity, the brain's ability to change and adapt as a result of experience and injury.

Sneezing Speed

When a person sneezes, the air along with droplets is expelled from the nose and mouth at a high speed. This speed can vary between individuals and sneezes, but it is estimated to be around 100 miles (160 km) per hour. Some estimates even put this speed higher. This rapid expulsion of air helps to effectively clear the nasal passages of irritants such as dust, pollen, or other foreign particles. The speed of a sneeze can cause droplets to travel a significant distance. On average, sneeze droplets can travel anywhere from 5 to 30 feet (1.5 to 9 meters), depending on the force of the sneeze and environmental conditions like humidity and air currents. This ability to travel long distances is why sneezing is a key factor in the spread of respiratory infectious diseases, emphasizing the importance of covering one's mouth to prevent the spread of pathogens.

Human Body

The percentage of water in our body is about 60%, this is greater than half of a person. Our lungs' airways would cover an area around the size of a tennis court if we spread them out flat. The largest organ in our body is our skin. There are about eighty-six billion neurons or nerve cells in our brain. When we are asleep, our brain is more active than when we are awake throughout the day. Our eyes are so sensitive that we could detect a candle flame in the dark from miles away. Our gastric lining regenerates every few days to avoid digesting itself, as it produces strong acids to help break down food. We get a new set of taste buds every 10 to 14 days. This keeps our sense of taste sharp to enjoy all our favorite foods.

Tongue Print

Just like fingerprints, everyone's tongue print is unique. Tongue prints are formed before we are born and stay the same our whole life. No two people have the same tongue print. Our tongue has a special pattern made up of ridges, lines, and bumps. These patterns are different for every person. These patterns are determined by our genes, which is why they are unique to each person.

Taste Buds' Lifespan

The tiny taste buds on your tongue have a very short lifespan. They only last about 10 to 14 days before they are replaced with new ones. This regeneration process ensures that the sense of taste remains functional throughout a person's life. Taste buds are small sensory organs on your tongue that allow you to experience different tastes like sweet, salty, sour, bitter and savory. Each taste bud contains several taste receptor cells, which are responsible for detecting these flavors. As people age, the rate of taste bud regeneration can slow down, which may contribute to changes in taste perception in older adults.

Electrical Power of the Human Brain

In addition to its remarkable capacity for thought and imagination, the human brain functions similarly to a tiny power plant inside your skull. Your brain produces approximately twenty watts of electrical power. That is sufficient energy to turn on a dim lightbulb. The billions of neurons that make up the brain are what provide its electrical energy. These neurons exchange messages with one another chemically and electrically. The brain is remarkably energy efficient for such a complex organ. Though it comprises only 2% of the body's mass, it consumes about 20% of the body's total energy.

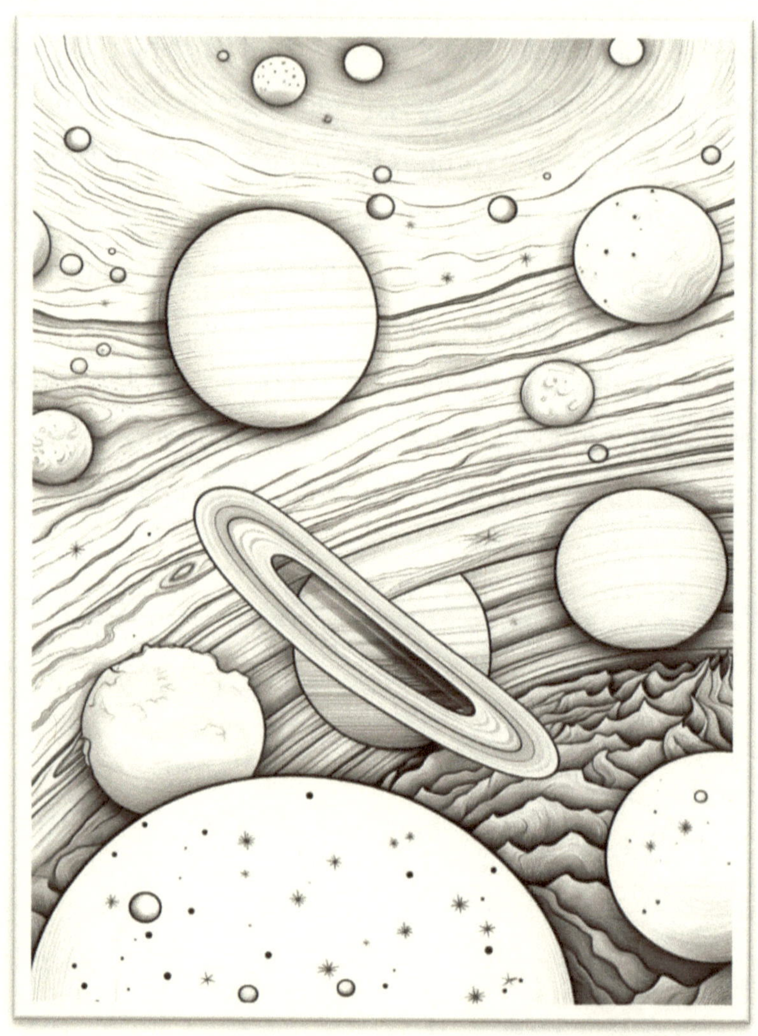

The Sun

Over a million Earths could fit inside the sun due to its immense size. With temperatures that can approach 27 million degrees Fahrenheit (15 million degrees Celsius), the Sun's core is incredibly hot. At about 9,932 degrees Fahrenheit (5,500 degrees Celsius). According to researchers, it is a middle-aged star, having reached a mass of approximately 4.6 billion years. Its hydrogen fuel will last for an additional 5 billion years, during which time it will transform into a red giant and then a white dwarf.

Mercury's Iron Core

Mercury's core is unusually large relative to its overall size. Unlike Earth, where the core makes up about one-third of the planet's total volume, Mercury's core accounts for approximately 85% of its radius. This suggests that Mercury has a disproportionately large iron core, a unique feature among the rocky planets in our solar system. There is strong evidence to suggest that Mercury's iron core is not entirely solid but has a partially molten layer. The existence of its magnetic field implies that there must be a liquid layer within its large iron core where this dynamo action can occur. The discovery of Mercury's magnetic field by Mariner 10 in the 1970s was a significant surprise to astronomers, as it challenged previous assumptions about the planet's internal structure.

Saturn's Rings are Not Solid

Saturn's rings are made up of innumerable tiny particles, ranging in size from dust grains to bigger pieces spanning several meters, instead of solid structures. With certain rocky components attached, the majority of these particles are composed of water and ice. The reflecting quality of the ice is responsible for the rings' brilliant look. From a distance, the rings appear to be a solid structure due to the dispersion of these particles; nevertheless, they are actually a large, dispersed collection of these pieces of rock and ice orbiting Saturn.

Neptune's Supersonic Winds

Neptune boasts some of the fastest winds in the solar system, with speeds reaching up to 1,300 miles (2,100 kilometers) per hour. These wind speeds are supersonic, meaning they exceed the speed of sound. This is particularly remarkable considering Neptune's distance from the Sun and relatively low solar energy input. The high velocity of Neptune's winds makes them faster than any other planetary winds in the solar system, surpassing even the swift winds observed on gas giants like Jupiter and Saturn.

Martian Summit

Mars is home to Olympus Mons, the tallest volcanic mountain in the solar system. This shield volcano reaches an astonishing height of about 13.6 miles (22km) above the Martian surface, dwarfing Mount Everest, Earth's highest mountain above sea level. Olympus Mons is not only tall but also incredibly wide, spanning approximately 373 miles (600km) in diameter, which is roughly equivalent to the size of the state of Arizona. Its immense size is partly due to the lower gravity on Mars, which allows geological formations to reach greater heights than they could on Earth.

Pluto's Heart-Shaped Glacier

The heart-shaped feature on Pluto, known as Tombaugh Regio, is one of the dwarf planet's most distinctive characteristics. This large, bright area measures approximately 990 miles (1,590km) across at its widest point. Named after Clyde Tombaugh, the astronomer who discovered Pluto in 1930, this region captured widespread attention when the New Horizons spacecraft provided detailed images during its flyby in 2015. The western lobe of Tombaugh Regio, called Sputnik Planitia, is particularly notable as it is a vast glacier composed mainly of nitrogen ice mixed with smaller amounts of methane and carbon monoxide.

Asteroid Belt's Missing Planet

The Asteroid Belt, located between Mars and Jupiter, has long been a subject of curiosity and speculation, particularly regarding the theory of a missing planet. Early astronomical theories, particularly the Titius-Bode law, suggested a certain regularity in the distances of planets from the Sun. However, instead of a planet, this region is filled with numerous small rocky bodies known as asteroids. This discrepancy led to the idea that perhaps a planet that once existed in this location was shattered or failed to form, leaving behind the debris that makes up the Asteroid Belt.

Jupiter's massive storm

Jupiter, the largest planet in our solar system, has a unique feature called the Great Red Spot. It is a gigantic storm; much bigger than any storm we have on Earth. In fact, it is so large that about three Earths could fit inside it. Astronomers have been observing the Great Red Spot for at least 400 years, but it could have been around for even longer. The Great Red Spot is a high-pressure area, kind of like a hurricane on Earth, but much larger and more powerful. It whirls around in the atmosphere of Jupiter, with winds reaching speeds of about 26-423 miles (430-680km) per hour.

Shooting Stars

When space rock or dust particles approach Earth's atmosphere, they burn up and become meteors, which are what we call shooting stars. They start off as little particles of metal or rock in orbit, known as meteoroids, and vaporize because of heat from friction with the air as they enter Earth's atmosphere, turning into meteors. As the hot rock is zipping through the atmosphere, the burning hot air is what creates the dazzling streak of light that a shooting star emits.

Space Dog Cosmonauts

During the 1950s and 1960s the Soviet space program used dogs to orbit space to determine whether human spaceflight was possible. Laika, a Soviet space dog, was the very first living creature to orbit the Earth. She made history in 1957, and her journey opened the door for human space exploration. Before their space missions, dogs went through rigorous training. They learned to endure the conditions of space, like the sensation of weightlessness and the loud sounds of rocket launches. Space dogs also wore specially designed spacesuits to protect them in space.

Venus: A World Where Days Outlast Years

A day on Venus, which is the duration of one complete rotation on its axis, is exceptionally long. This is believed to be the longest rotation of any planet in the Solar System. It takes about 243 Earth days for Venus to complete a single rotation. This duration is even longer than a year on Venus which is about 225 Earth days. So, a day on Venus ends up being longer than a year on Venus.

The Scent of the Moon

The smell of the Moon is a unique topic, primarily based on the accounts of astronauts who have visited the lunar surface during the Apollo missions. Astronauts who walked on the Moon during the Apollo missions reported that lunar dust, once brought inside the spacecraft and exposed to air, smelled similar to spent gunpowder. This description was consistent among several Apollo astronauts. The smell is thought to be a result of the lunar regolith, moon dust, composed of silicates that might react in the presence of oxygen and moisture in the spacecraft to produce this peculiar odor. It is important to note that the Moon itself does not have a smell, as it lacks an atmosphere.

Galactic Cannibalism

Galactic cannibalism occurs when a larger galaxy, due to its stronger gravitational pull, merges with and absorbs a smaller galaxy. This process is a natural part of the evolution of galaxies and plays a significant role in their growth and morphological changes over billions of years. During these interactions, the stars of the smaller galaxy are either assimilated into the larger galaxy or flung out into space. The central super massive black holes of the galaxies can also merge, leading to the growth of some of the most massive black holes known in the universe. One of the outcomes of galactic cannibalism can be the formation of elliptical galaxies. While spiral galaxies like our Milky Way are characterized by flat, rotating disks, elliptical galaxies lack distinct features and have more randomized star orbits. Many elliptical galaxies are believed to have formed through the merging of two or more spiral galaxies. This process disrupts the ordered motion of the spiral galaxies, resulting in the more chaotic orbits of stars in elliptical galaxies. The Milky Way itself is predicted to eventually undergo a similar process, merging with the Andromeda galaxy in a few billion years.

The Color of the Universe

The average color of the universe, known as Cosmic Latte, is a pale, creamy shade of off-white. This color was determined by a team of astronomers from Johns Hopkins University in 2002. They analyzed light from over 200,000 galaxies within the observable universe to calculate the average color. Initially, the team thought the color would be turquoise but later corrected it to the current beige shade after accounting for a flaw in their analysis.

A Planet of Diamond

The concept of diamond planets is rooted in our understanding of carbon chemistry and physics under extreme conditions. In environments with high pressure and temperature, such as the interiors of certain exoplanets, carbon atoms can bond in a way that forms diamond. One of the most discussed examples of a potential diamond planet is 55 Cancri e. This exoplanet, which orbits a star in the constellation Cancer, is believed to have a carbon-rich composition. Scientists speculate that the intense pressure and heat in the planet's interior could transform this carbon into diamond, potentially making a significant portion of the planet's mass diamond-like.

Is Space Silent

Space is often perceived as completely silent due to the absence of a medium like air to carry sound waves. In the vacuum of space, sound, as we commonly understand it, cannot propagate. This means that traditional sound waves, which require a medium to travel through like air, water, or solids, cannot be heard in the vacuum of space. While space is void of sound in the conventional sense, it is not completely silent if one considers 'sound' more broadly. Astronomical objects and phenomena can emit radio waves and other forms of electromagnetic radiation that can be converted into sound. For example, scientists can translate radio signals or the interactions of charged particles into sound waves. These converted sounds offer us a different way to study and understand the universe.

Lunar Shadows

Shadows on the Moon are notably sharper and darker compared to those on Earth. This is primarily due to the lack of atmosphere on the Moon. Earth's atmosphere scatters light, which softens the edges of shadows and often fills them with diffused light. On the Moon, without an atmosphere to scatter sunlight, shadows are much more defined and contrasted. The transition from light to dark in lunar shadows is abrupt creating a stark distinction between illuminated and shaded areas. Another interesting aspect of lunar shadows is related to the lack of twilight on the Moon. On Earth, the atmosphere scatters and refracts sunlight, creating the effect of twilight, where the sky remains lit for a time even after the sun has set. However, on the Moon, when the sun sets, the sky goes from day to night almost instantly due to the absence of an atmosphere.

Rain of Iron

In some extreme exoplanetary environments, particularly on ultra-hot exoplanets, temperatures can be so high that metals like iron vaporize into the atmosphere. These exoplanets, often gas giants larger than Jupiter, can have day side temperatures exceeding thousands of degrees Fahrenheit/Celsius, hot enough to vaporize metals. On the cooler night side of these planets, the vaporized iron can condense into clouds and precipitate as iron rain. This phenomenon is a result of the extreme temperature differences between the day side and the night side of the planet.

Black Holes Sing

The concept of black holes 'singing' refers to the gravitational waves they produce, particularly when two black holes orbit each other and eventually merge. These gravitational waves are ripples in the fabric of spacetime caused by the immense gravitational forces at play. When detected and converted into sound waves, these signals can resemble a kind of 'chirping' sound, which increases in frequency and intensity as the black holes spiral closer together before merging. This phenomenon is often poetically described as the 'song' of black holes.

Uranus' Sideways Rotation

Because of its enormous axial tilt, Uranus is unlike any other planet in the solar system. Uranus's rotation axis is tilted by around 98 degrees with respect to its orbit, whereas most planets have very mild tilts in their axes of rotation. This indicates that the planet revolves on its side, with its poles at various points throughout its orbit facing nearly straight toward the Sun. Each pole thus receives around 42 years of nonstop sunlight, followed by an additional 42 years of darkness. The orientation of the other planets in the solar system is more upright than this strange rotation.

Solar Flip

The Sun's magnetic field reverses on a regular basis, about every 11 years, in accordance with its solar cycle. Because of the Sun's asymmetrical rotation, the equator rotates faster than the poles, the magnetic field gradually becomes more distorted during this cycle. The magnetic field lines eventually reach a point where they are so twisted that they 'snap' and reorganize themselves, switching the positions of the magnetic poles. Several decades of solar observations have revealed that this magnetic field reversal is a crucial component of the solar cycle.

Raining Diamonds

Both Saturn and Jupiter have extremely thick atmospheres full of carbon, which diamonds are made from. When lightning storms happen on these planets, the pressure and temperature increase drastically. This intense pressure can squash the carbon into graphite, and then even further into diamonds. As this process happens, it is similar to tiny diamonds falling through the sky.

Planet Venus

Venus is a very interesting planet in our solar system because it spins in a different way compared to most other planets, including Earth. It rotates in the opposite direction to most other planets in the solar system, a phenomenon known as retrograde rotation. So, on Venus, the Sun would rise in the west and set in the east. The reasons behind Venus's retrograde rotation are not entirely clear. One theory suggests that it could be due to a massive collision with another celestial body early in its history. It has an extremely slow rotation on its axis.

Zipper Name Origin

Compared to modern zippers, the device was more like an intricate hook-and-eye shoe fastener. American inventor Whitcomb L. Judson created it in the latter half of the 1800s. It eventually became the zipper because of the way he advertised it as a more straightforward and dependable shoe button substitute. The B.F. Goodrich Company first used the name zipper in 1923. The mechanism created a sound when it was operated, so the business decided to give it a memorable name, zipper, for its new line of rubber boots. Eventually, the name stayed, and these fasteners were referred to by their generic name. Over time, the zipper's construction and operation were refined.

Denim Jeans and Gold Miners

The creation of denim jeans is closely linked to the California Gold Rush in the mid-19th century. Miners needed sturdy and durable clothing that could withstand the harsh conditions of gold mining. Levi Strauss, a German immigrant, and Jacob Davis, a tailor, patented a design for pants made from denim and reinforced with rivets at the stress points, which made them exceptionally durable in 1873. These pants were ideal for miners who required tough, long-lasting workwear. Over time, these practical aspects made denim jeans popular not just among miners but also in other labor-intensive professions.

The Masculine Origins of High Heels

In the fifteenth century, men who rode horses in Persia, or modern-day Iran, designed the first high heels. The high heel's utilitarian design served to keep the rider's feet firmly in the stirrups, especially when the rider stood up to shoot arrows. Persian soldiers and nobility grew to associate this look with strength and status. Early in the 17th century, European nobles embraced the high heel as a fashion statement when Persian officials traveled there. The heels were regarded as a symbol of upper-class and masculine status. European men, such as France's King Louis XIV, advocated wearing high heels with formal wear. Over time, the trend of high heels moved into women's fashion, and by the 18th century, they had become primarily associated with women's clothing.

Victorian Black Clothing

In Victorian times, black clothing was strongly associated with mourning. The death of Prince Albert in 1861 prompted Queen Victoria to wear black for the rest of her life, setting a societal trend. Mourning attire, especially for women, involved strict guidelines and could last for extended periods, sometimes up to several years, depending on the deceased's relation to the mourner. This practice made black clothing a common sight in Victorian society. Technological advancements in textile dyeing also influenced this. This made black clothing more accessible and practical, as it was less likely to fade with washing and wear. As a result, black garments became a staple of Victorian fashion, worn not only for mourning but also for everyday wear by both men and women.

Silk's Royal Status in China

Silk was so valuable in ancient China that it was only allowed to be used by the royal family and the highest social classes for many generations. This served to uphold social hierarchy as well as serve as a symbol of riches and power. Wearing silk was a privilege bestowed to the emperor's court and other dignitaries, while the process of producing it remained a state secret. Silk's uniqueness improved its standing not only in China but also abroad, where it became a highly prized luxury commodity. Particularly along the Silk Road, a network of trade routes that connected China to the Middle East, Africa, and other continents, silk played a key role in China's diplomacy and international trade. Chinese emperors often used silk as a prestigious diplomatic gift to make alliances and display their wealth and cultural superiority.

18th Century Wig Scenting

The main reason for scenting wigs in the 18th century was to mask unpleasant odors. During this era, personal hygiene practices were quite different from today's standards, and regular washing of hair was not a common practice. Wigs, often made from human, horse, or goat hair, could absorb smells from the environment and from the wearer's own body. Perfuming these wigs helped to cover any bad smells and was considered a necessity for the fashionable elite. Scented powder and the perfumes that were used were often made from expensive and exotic ingredients, reflecting the wearer's wealth and status.

Ancient Egyptian Fashion

The most used fabric in ancient Egyptian clothing was linen, made from the flax plant that grew abundantly along the Nile River. Linen was favored due to its light and breathable qualities, which were ideal in the hot and arid Egyptian climate. The quality of the linen varied, with the wealthier classes wearing finer, more delicate linen, while the lower classes wore coarser grades. Cotton, another popular fabric today, was not known in Egypt until the first millennium BCE. Fashion in ancient Egypt was not just about style or comfort, it was deeply intertwined with social status and religious symbolism. Pharaohs and high-ranking officials often wore elaborately decorated garments and headdresses, symbolizing their power and divine status. Jewelry was also an important aspect of Egyptian fashion, with both men and women adorning themselves with necklaces, bracelets, earrings, and rings. Jewelry was believed to offer protection and had significant religious and symbolic meaning.

FAMOUS BUILDINGS AROUND THE GLOBE

Eiffel Tower

The Eiffel Tower, located in Paris, France, is one of the most recognizable structures in the world. Completed in 1889 for the Exposition Universelle (World's Fair) to celebrate the 100th anniversary of the French Revolution, it was designed by the engineer Gustave Eiffel's company. Originally criticized by some of France's leading artists and intellectuals for its design, the Eiffel Tower has become a global cultural icon of France and a symbol of architectural artistry and ingenuity. Standing at 1,063 feet (324 meters) tall, it was the tallest man-made structure in the world until the completion of the Chrysler Building in New York City in 1930.

Leaning Tower of Pisa

The tower is in Pisa, a city in the Tuscany region of Italy. Construction of the tower began in 1173 and took nearly 200 years to complete, spanning across three stages. The tower began to lean during its construction in the 12th century, due to an inadequate foundation on soft ground. The lean has been gradually increasing until recent efforts to stabilize it. It is a freestanding bell tower of the cathedral of the Italian city of Pisa, known worldwide for its unintended tilt. It is a prime example of Romanesque architecture, particularly in its use of columns and arches. The tower stands about 184 feet (56 meters) tall and has 294 steps leading up to the top.

Empire State Building

The Empire State Building, located in New York City, USA, is an iconic skyscraper and a marvel of 20th-century architecture. Completed in 1931, it stood as the world's tallest building for nearly 40 years until the North Tower of the World Trade Center was completed in 1970. The building rises to a total height of 1,454 feet (443.2 meters), including its antenna. Designed in the Art Deco style, it has been a defining feature of the New York City skyline, admired for its distinctive, streamlined appearance and its majestic spire.

Great Wall of China

The Great Wall of China is an extensive series of fortifications built along the historical northern borders of China. The earliest sections were constructed over several centuries, dating back to the 7th century BC. The most famous and well-preserved parts were built during the Ming Dynasty. The wall's primary purpose was to protect Chinese states and empires from invasions and raids by various nomadic groups from the Eurasian Steppe. Stretching approximately 13,171 miles (21,196 km), it is often hailed as one of the most impressive architectural feats in history.

Lotus Temple

The Lotus Temple, located in New Delhi, India, is renowned for its remarkable lotus flower-like design. Completed in 1986, the temple was designed by Iranian architect Fariborz Sahba and has won numerous architectural awards. The structure is composed of 27 free-standing marble-clad petals arranged in clusters to form nine sides, with nine doors opening onto a central hall capable of holding up to 2,500 people. The design is inspired by the lotus flower, which is a symbol of purity and peace, embodying the key Bahá'í principle of unity. The Lotus Temple is a Bahá'í House of Worship, notable for its open-arm approach to all religions.

Louvre

The largest art museum in the world, the Louvre is situated in Paris, France, and has a long and illustrious history. During the French Revolution, Philip II had the Louvre converted from a fortification to a public museum in the late 12th century. With an exhibition of 537 paintings when it first opened in 1793, it has expanded to accommodate some 380,000 artifacts and 35,000 pieces of art across more than 60,600 square meters of exhibition area.

Chrysler Building

The Chrysler Building, located in New York City, USA, is a renowned example of Art Deco architecture and one of the most iconic skyscrapers in the world. Designed by architect William Van Alen, the building was completed in 1930. It stands at a height of 1,046 feet (319 meters), including its distinctive stainless-steel spire. The building was briefly the world's tallest building, surpassing the Eiffel Tower, before being overtaken by the Empire State Building in 1931. The Chrysler Building is celebrated for its unique terraced crown, composed of seven radiating terraced arches, and its ornamentation reflecting the automotive industry, in line with the Chrysler Corporation's identity.

Taj Mahal

The Taj Mahal's construction began around 1632 and was largely completed in 1648, with the surrounding structures and garden finalized five years later. It is estimated that over 20,000 artisans and laborers were involved in its construction, hailing from various regions and countries including Persia, the Ottoman Empire, and Europe, reflecting the Mughal Empire's extensive reach and influence. Skilled craftsmen were brought in for specialized tasks, such as inlay work and stone carving. Materials were sourced from all over India and central Asia, and it is said that over 1,000 elephants were used to transport these materials. This diverse workforce and the vast array of materials used, highlight the Taj Mahal's status as a symbol of the Mughal Empire's wealth and architectural ambition.

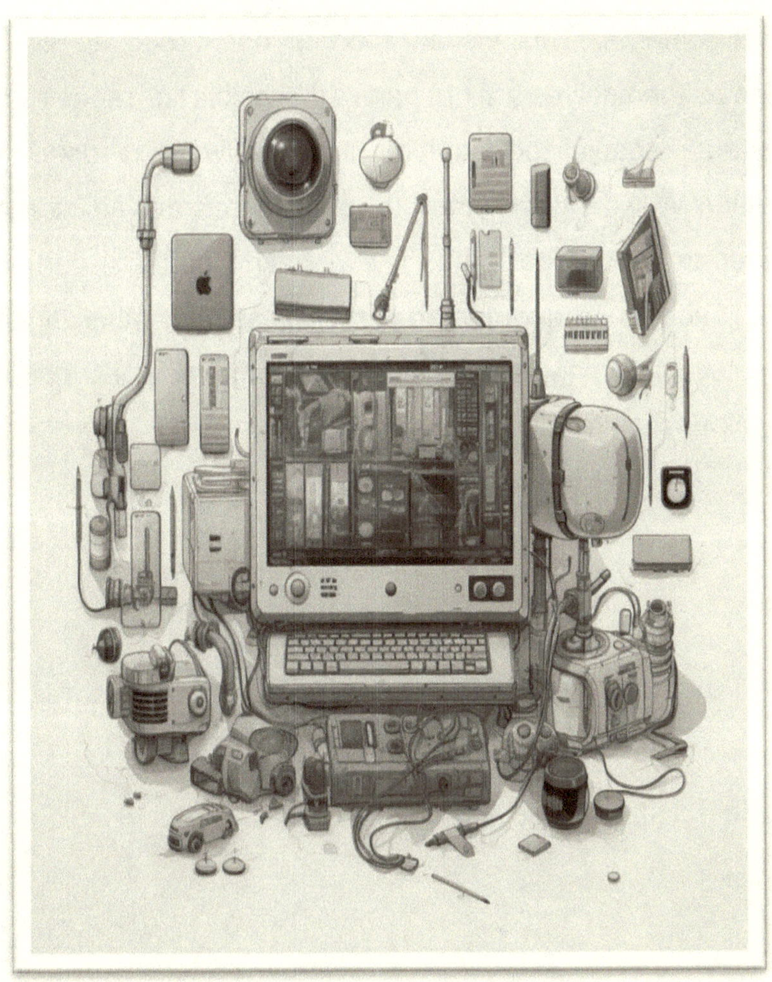

Wi-Fi: Visible Connections

The concept of visualizing Wi-Fi signal patterns with special glasses stems from research and technological experiments that convert the invisible signals into visible light patterns. This visualization is not direct, as Wi-Fi signals themselves are not part of the visible light spectrum. Instead, specialized equipment or software is used to detect Wi-Fi signal strength and then translate these readings into visual data. The resulting patterns can be displayed using augmented reality glasses or other digital displays, allowing users to see the strength and distribution of Wi-Fi signals in their environment.

Robotic Rivalry

One of the most well-known sports played with robots is robot soccer, also known as RoboCup. This international robotics competition aims to advance the field of robotics and artificial intelligence through the challenge of soccer. Teams of robots are programmed to play soccer against each other, testing their abilities in movement, decision-making, and teamwork. The goal of the RoboCup initiative is by the mid-21st century to develop a team of fully autonomous humanoid robot soccer players that can win against the human world champion team in soccer, pushing the boundaries of robotics and AI research.

Digital Ink

Many e-readers use a technology known as electronic ink or e-ink to display content. Unlike traditional LCD screens found in smartphones and computers, e-ink displays utilize actual ink particles to create their images. These microscopic particles are suspended in a clear fluid within a thin film, allowing them to be manipulated electronically. When an electric charge is applied, the ink particles rearrange themselves to form text and images, mimicking the appearance of ink on paper. This technology is especially valued for its paper-like readability and low glare, making it easier on the eyes and readable in direct sunlight.

Galactic Pioneers

One of the earliest known video games, Spacewar, predates human spaceflight. Developed in 1962 by Steve Russell and others at the Massachusetts Institute of Technology, Spacewar was a two-player game where each player controlled a spaceship and attempted to destroy the other's ship while maneuvering around a central gravitational well. This game was created more than a year before Soviet cosmonaut Yuri Gagarin became the first human to journey into outer space in April 1961.

Artistic Endeavors of Artificial Intelligence

Artificial intelligence (AI) has created works of art ranging from paintings and drawings to music and literature, making substantial advances into the artistic community. Neural networks, complex algorithms that can recognize patterns and styles in previously created artwork, are used to do this. Artificial intelligence (AI) systems that can evaluate thousands of works of art and train to create new works that are frequently identical to works of human art include Generative Adversarial Networks (GANs) and deep learning models. These AI-generated works of art can be completely unique, or they can imitate well-known artists' techniques.

The First Computer Mouse

Douglas Engelbart created the first computer mouse in 1964, and it was made of wood. American engineer and inventor Engelbart was a trailblazer around human-computer interaction. It was just a regular-sized wooden block with a single button on top that resembled a matchbox. It could roll on the surface thanks to two metal wheels on the bottom of it; the motion was translated into movement of the cursor on the computer screen. In 1968, the mouse and a graphical user interface were first shown in public. Since the cord exiting the back of the model resembled the tail of a mouse, the device was dubbed a 'mouse.' Many revisions have been made to the original mouse design.

Smartphones

The computers used for the Apollo 11 moon landing were not as powerful as the typical smartphone. The smartphone may be small, but it is jam-packed with a ton of useful features. The Apollo 11 computer took up an entire room due to its size. The smartphone has quick thinking and memory and compared to the outdated Apollo 11 computer, it can perform calculations and recall information far more quickly. Beautiful images and colors can be displayed on the screen of your smartphone. Apollo 11's outdated computer was limited to displaying basic black-and-white images, much like a vintage television. The smartphone is incredibly multifunctional, can be used for gaming, taking pictures, browsing the internet, and even making video calls.

The First Video Game

Most people agree that Tennis for Two, which physicist William Higinbotham made in 1958, was the first video game. This came about long before the incredibly detailed graphics and intricate gameplay of modern video games. Ping pong or tennis at a reduced difficulty was replicated in the game. Players adjusted the shot angle with a knob and hit the ball with a button, all while viewing a two-dimensional side view of a tennis court. To control the angle of their shot and try to play the ball over the net, players utilized a small box with buttons and rotating dials. There was only one dot that bounced back and forth in the game, which was shown on a small circular oscilloscope screen.

Banksy's Secret Identity

Banksy, the notorious street artist known for his political and social commentary art, has successfully kept his identity a secret. Over the years, there have been numerous speculations and investigations into Banksy's identity, to no avail. His ability to remain unidentified adds to the intrigue of his work and aligns with the anti-establishment and subversive nature of his art. By staying anonymous, Banksy challenges traditional notions of fame and the commercialization of art, making it a critical component of his overall artistic expression.

Lady Gaga's Meat Dress

In addition to being a daring design statement, Lady Gaga's meat dress served as a vehicle for political protest. She clarified in an interview that the clothing was a protest against the "Don't Ask, Don't Tell" policy of the US military, which at the time prohibited openly gay individuals from enlisting. Gaga wanted to emphasize the value of standing up for what one believes in and the requirement that everyone has rights by donning the outfit. Following its premiere, the meat dress was preserved as a sort of jerky by taxidermists and went on show at the Rock and Roll Hall of Fame as a part of the Women Who Rock exhibit. The uncooked beef was changed into a kind of leather through the preservation process, guaranteeing it could be preserved for years.

David Lynch's Weather Reports

David Lynch, known for his distinctive and surreal approach to filmmaking, brings a similar style to his daily weather reports. These reports, which he posts on his YouTube channel, are far from the typical meteorological updates. Lynch delivers the weather forecasts in his own enigmatic and contemplative style, often against a backdrop of peculiar objects or settings that evoke the mood of his cinematic works. His reports are brief, usually lasting only a minute or two, and often include personal remarks or observations, making them a blend of weather information and a glimpse into Lynch's creative world. This consistent ritual has turned his weather reports into a daily moment of Zen for many followers, further cementing Lynch's status as a unique figure in both the realms of cinema and now, quirky online content.

Ai Weiwei's Sunflower Seeds

Ai Weiwei's 'Sunflower Seeds' installation, showcased in the Tate Modern's Turbine Hall in 2010, was a monumental display consisting of over 100 million individually hand-crafted porcelain sunflower seeds. Each seed was painstakingly sculpted and painted by skilled artisans from the town of Jingdezhen in China, known for its history in porcelain making. The project took several years to complete, involving over 1,600 artisans. The sheer scale of the installation was a critical element of the work, commenting on the vastness of China's population and the labor-intensive processes prevalent in the country's manufacturing sector.

Marina Abramović's Silent Stare

Marina Abramović's 'The Artist is Present' was performed at the Museum of Modern Art in New York City in 2010. Abramović sat silently for about 2.5 months, in the museum's atrium while visitors were invited to sit directly across from her and engage in non-verbal interaction. This performance marked the longest duration for which Abramović had ever performed a single piece. Each day, she maintained her position from the moment the museum opened until it closed, embodying the extreme discipline and endurance for which she was known.

Jeff Koons' Balloon Animals

Balloon Animals by Jeff Koons is a piece from his Celebration series, which he started making in the late nineties. These sculptures are made of highly polished stainless steel with a translucent color coating, emulating the shapes of twisted balloon animals, which are a common sight at children's parties. One characteristic of Koons' approach is the way he can take a basic thing and turn it into a large-scale, enduring piece of art. The sculptures are startling in scale; for instance 'Balloon Dog (Orange)' is more than ten feet tall. These sculptures' mirror-finish surfaces reflect the surrounding area and onlookers, producing a dynamic and participatory visual experience.

Wrapping Projects

One of Christo and Jeanne-Claude's most famous projects was the wrapping of the Reichstag in Berlin in 1995. This monumental undertaking involved covering the entire German Parliament building with silver fabric and blue ropes. The preparation for this project took almost 24 years, with various political and legal hurdles that the artists had to overcome. The actual wrapping took two weeks, and the fabric remained in place for 14 days. This project was significant not only for its sheer scale but also for its symbolic value, especially in post-Cold War Germany. The Reichstag, with its historical baggage, was transformed into an artistic spectacle, prompting a re-examination of its symbolic meaning and the role of art in public spaces.

STRANGE & WONDERFUL FURNITURE

Most Expensive Chair in the World

The 'Dragon's Chair' by Eileen Gray is a remarkable example of Art Deco furniture and her craft. The chair, which was designed between 1917 and 1919, is distinguished by its unusual shape and the eye-catching depiction of two interwoven dragons that serve as the armrests. The dragons are expertly portrayed in lacquered wood, a medium and method that Gray especially enjoyed, demonstrating her ability to blend traditional workmanship with a postmodern design. In addition to being a beautiful piece, the chair is also an important piece in the history of modern furniture design because of Gray's interest in both decorative arts and utilitarian design.

Ancient Egyptians Invented the Folding Chair

In ancient Egypt, folding chairs were not merely functional items; they were symbols of status and luxury. These chairs were often made from precious materials like wood, ivory, or even gold, and were beautifully decorated with intricate carvings and inlays. Their use was generally reserved for the pharaohs and high-ranking officials, reflecting their high status in society. The craftsmanship involved in making these chairs was highly advanced for the time, indicating the skill and artistry of Egyptian artisans. The chairs were designed to be both practical for travel and visually impressive, showcasing the wealth and power of their owners.

Furniture in Space

In the microgravity environment of the International Space Station (ISS), traditional beds are not feasible, so astronauts use specially designed sleep stations. These stations are similar in size to a phone booth and are equipped with a sleeping bag attached to the wall. Astronauts secure themselves in these bags to prevent floating around while they sleep. The sleep stations also serve as personal spaces for the astronauts, equipped with personal items like photos, small personal belongings, and even a window in some cases. This arrangement is crucial not only for the physical rest of the astronauts but also for their psychological well-being, providing a semblance of privacy and personal space in the confined environment of the space station. To cope with the challenges of living in a microgravity environment, much of the furniture and equipment on the ISS, including workstations and dining areas, is covered with Velcro. This allows astronauts to secure themselves, their tools, and their food packets to prevent them from floating away. Magnets are also used for some objects. For example, utensils and trays might have magnetic properties to stick to the tables. This innovative use of Velcro and magnets is essential for day-to-day activities in space.

Hidden Compartments

The popularity of furniture with hidden compartments during the 18th and 19th centuries can be seen as a reflection of the societal trends and concerns of the time. In an era marked by political upheavals, espionage, and the burgeoning of private societies, such secretive features in furniture provided a means of securing confidential documents, valuables, or personal items. Craftsmen skilled in cabinetry and joinery developed intricate mechanisms and clever designs to conceal these compartments. This trend was not only practical but also catered to the intrigue and fascination with secrecy and privacy that was prevalent among the elite and intellectual circles of the time.

Coffee Table's Evolution

The coffee table, as we know it today, evolved from the tea table, which was prevalent in Europe, particularly in Britain, during the late 18th and early 19th centuries. Originally, tea tables were taller, resembling what we would consider side tables or small dining tables today. They were used primarily in the tea-drinking rituals that were a significant part of social and domestic life. As coffee gained popularity and the practice of drinking it in living rooms or lounges became more common, the design of the table adapted. By the 20th century, the tea table transformed into the lower coffee table, designed to be accessible for people seated in lounge chairs or sofas, facilitating casual conversation and the serving of coffee.

Rocking Chairs & Health Benefits

Rocking chairs are more than just cozy furniture because they have been connected to several health advantages. Rocking has a rhythmic motion that has been shown to reduce stress because it can have a calming, meditation-like effect. Additionally, by moving gently and steadily, you can enhance blood flow throughout your body and promote circulation. Furthermore, studies have demonstrated that rocking helps people with back pain and arthritis by lowering discomfort and increasing mobility. Rocking chairs are a useful tool for new moms as they help soothe babies and encourage healthier sleeping habits for both the parent and the child.

Cultural Significance of African Stools

In many African cultures, stools are more than mere furniture; they are potent symbols of authority and status. Particularly in West African societies, such as among the Akan people of Ghana, stools are often associated with chieftaincy and royalty. They are considered to embody the soul of the leader and, by extension, the soul of the people he governs. The design of these stools is highly significant and often includes symbolic motifs and carvings that represent the beliefs, history, and values of the community. The stool's connection to leadership is so profound that the enthronement of a new chief or king often involves a ceremony where he is seated on a traditional stool, signifying his acceptance of the responsibilities of leadership.

Pink Cars and Their Rarity

Pink cars, due to their rarity, often carry unique cultural and social associations. In many societies, pink is often stereotypically associated with femininity, which influences the perception of pink cars. However, in recent years, this perception has been challenged, and pink cars are increasingly seen as a statement of individuality and personal style, regardless of gender. Moreover, pink cars are often used in promotional campaigns or for special occasions due to their standout color, making them ideal for attracting attention. They are frequently seen in charitable events, particularly those related to breast cancer awareness, where pink plays a significant symbolic role.

Car with the Most Mileage

Owner of the 1966 Volvo P1800, Irv Gordon, drove the vehicle for more than 50 years, traveling an incredible distance, after buying it brand-new in 1966. Gordon was a Long Island, New York, educator who loved to drive and took good care of his vehicle, which extended its life. His commitment to his Volvo P1800 went beyond simple driving; it was evidence of his appreciation for high standards of excellence and the necessity of routine maintenance. In terms of the most distance in a personally owned, non-commercial car, he broke the Guinness World Record. Gordon had become a legend among auto enthusiasts and an inspiration for proper long-term vehicle care by the time he had accumulated over 3 million kilometers.

Cars Outnumbering People

With its vast road network and spreading metropolitan design, Los Angeles is well-known for having one of the highest rates of car ownership and usage worldwide. The total population of the city has been exceeded by the number of registered automobiles on several occasions throughout its history. Los Angeles's distinct feature stems from its urban planning and development patterns, which have significantly prioritized private vehicle mobility above public transportation alternatives. The broad roadways and ample parking lots that characterize the city's infrastructure indicate how dependent the city is on automobiles for transportation. The overwhelming number of cars in the city has shaped Los Angeles' culture and way of life, impacting everything from daily life to urban planning.

Floating Car

The Amphicar, manufactured in Germany from 1961 to 1968, was a pioneering vehicle designed for both land and water operation. It was powered by a Triumph Herald four-cylinder engine that drove the rear wheels on land and two propellers when in water. The Amphicar had a unique door sealing system to keep it watertight when transitioning into the water. With a top speed of about 70 mph (113 km/h) on land and 7 mph (11 km/h) in water, it wasn't particularly fast in either domain but offered the unique ability to switch between being a car and a boat. Its amphibious nature made it a popular novelty vehicle and a remarkable example of innovative automotive engineering in the mid-20th century.

Secret Behind New Car Smell

The characteristic 'new car smell' that many people find appealing is actually a result of a mix of volatile organic compounds (VOCs). These compounds are emitted from various materials used in car manufacturing, such as plastics, adhesives, upholstery, and carpeting. Some of the common chemicals that contribute to this smell include benzene, formaldehyde, and toluene, among others. These substances gradually off-gas over time, diminishing the intensity of the smell. The scent is particularly strong in brand-new cars as these chemicals have had little time to dissipate.

Finland's Wife-Carrying Championship

This quirky event takes place annually in Sonkajärvi, Finland. The origin of the competition is based on an old Finnish legend. It's said that a bandit named Herkko Rosvo-Ronkainen lived in the forest and trained his thieves by carrying heavy sacks on their backs, which eventually evolved into the idea of carrying women. In the competition, the course which is about 850 feet (253.5m) long, includes various obstacles like water and hurdles. The couples can choose from several carrying styles, like the classic piggyback, the fireman's carry (over the shoulder), or the most popular, the "Estonian carry," where the wife hangs upside-down, her legs around the husband's shoulders and holding onto his waist. The prize is the wife's weight in beer.

Italy's Orange-Throwing Festival

Known as the Battle of the Oranges, it is a unique and lively event that is part of the Ivrea Carnival, which occurs every year. The festival has its roots in the medieval history of Ivrea. It is said to commemorate a rebellion against tyranny in the 12th century. According to legend, the rebellion started when a young woman refused the local duke's 'right' to spend a night with every newlywed bride, sparking an uprising. So, the orange-throwing battle symbolizes the fight against oppression. Participants are divided into a group that represents the guards of the tyrant and the other the commoners. The event is well-organized with safety measures in place and only designated throwers are allowed, and spectators are advised to wear protective gear or stand in designated safe zones.

Norway's Night Sun Soccer Match

Usually in late June, around the time of the Summer Solstice, the match takes place in northern Norway. It takes advantage of the Midnight Sun, which is a summertime natural phenomenon that happens north of the Arctic Circle. During this time, the sun can still be seen at midnight and all through the night. This match is special because, although it starts late at night, it continues throughout the daytime. The natural lighting for the game is provided by the sun remaining above the horizon. In addition to other Midnight Sun events, the soccer match draws tourists to northern Norway by giving them the opportunity to witness the bizarre and breathtaking phenomenon of perpetual daylight.

World Pea Shooting Championships

In England, the World Pea Shooting Championships were first held in 1971. The purpose of the event was to raise money for the village hall in the area. Every year, competitors from all over the world travel to the championships to compete in this exceptional event. Pea shooters are used by rivals to shoot peas at a target. The standard distance to the target is 12 feet (3.66 meters). Shooting at a soft target makes it easier to score because it allows the peas to stick during the competition. Pea shooters are typically made of simple tubes, usually made of plastic or metal. To increase accuracy and range, rivals have, nevertheless, created more advanced and specialized shooters over time. To maintain fairness, the peas used in the championship are standardized.

Cheese Rolling Festival

This festival, which takes place at Cooper's Hill in England, is famous worldwide. It involves rolling a large wheel of cheese down a steep hill with people racing after it. A round cheese, typically a Double Gloucester, which weighs about 9lb (4kg), is rolled from the top of Cooper's Hill and participants race downhill after it. The first person to cross the finish line is the winner, who gets to take home the cheese. Cooper's Hill is extremely steep and uneven, making the races dangerous. Participants often tumble, roll, and somersault down the hill, resulting in a mix of excitement and injuries. Despite this, the event draws many enthusiastic competitors and spectators every year.

Ostrich Races

Ostriches are the fastest birds on land and can reach speeds up to 45 miles (72km). Their long legs allow them to cover significant ground quickly, making ostrich races fast paced and exciting to watch. In ostrich races, riders sit on specially designed saddles and hold onto handles while perched on the ostrich's back. These races are typically held in certain regions where ostriches are farmed or found in abundance. The ostriches used in races are typically trained, but given their natural disposition, they can be unpredictable, adding an element of challenge to the races.

World Worm Charming Championships

The World Worm Charming Championships originated in a village in Cheshire, England in 1980. The aim of the competition is to charm as many earthworms out of the ground as possible within a set time limit, without digging or using water. Participants referred to as worm charmers, are given a small plot of land. They use different techniques to encourage worms to the surface. This can include tapping, playing music, and vibrating the soil. The methods are often creative and vary widely among participants. The idea is that the vibrations make the worms think it's raining or that a predator is coming, so they come to the surface. Each team has 30 minutes to charm as many worms as possible. The worms are then counted, and the team with the most worms wins. After the competition, the worms are carefully returned to the ground.

Pumpkin Regatta

The Pumpkin Regatta is a race where people hollow out giant pumpkins, which can weigh hundreds of pounds (kilograms), and use them as boats to paddle across a body of water. This competition is held in many countries around the world. Participants often dressed in costumes, sit in their carved-out pumpkins and paddle these pumpkin boats using oars across a set course on a lake or river. These pumpkins are a special type of pumpkin, known as the Atlantic

Mobile Phone Throwing Championship

The Mobile Phone Throwing World Championships originated in Finland in the 2000s. The objective of the competition is to throw a mobile phone as far and as accurately as possible. While participants can bring their own phones, organizers usually provide standardized phones to ensure fairness. These phones are often older models, which are heavier and thus more challenging to throw. The event also promotes recycling. The phones used are typically old or broken, and they are properly recycled after the event. What started in Finland has spread to other countries, with similar events being organized around the world.

Toe Wrestling Championship

Toe wrestling is a quirky and lesser-known sport, but it has its own set of enthusiasts and even championships. Toe wrestling first took place in the 1970s in Staffordshire, England. The sport is like arm wrestling. Two competitors lock their toes together and attempt to pin their opponent's foot down. Matches are played with the right foot first, then the left, and if needed, a decider with the right foot again. The World Toe Wrestling Championship has become an annual event that competitors from around the world participate in.

FAMOUS FESTIVALS AROUND THE WORLD

Carnival in Rio de Janeiro

One of the main attractions of the Rio Carnival is the Samba Parade, held in the Sambadrome Marquês de Sapucaí. This parade features a competition among the samba schools of Rio. These schools are large, neighborhood-based organizations that work year-round to prepare for the Carnival. Their preparations include creating elaborate floats and costumes, and choreographing dance routines. The samba schools are judged on various elements, including theme, music, costumes, and the quality of their samba dancing. The Carnival in Rio has a rich history, with its roots tracing back to European festivals that were brought to Brazil. Over time, it incorporated African and indigenous cultural elements, particularly through the influence of samba music, which has African origins. The festival is not just a massive party but also a reflection of Brazilian culture, history, and social issues. Themes chosen by samba schools for their parades often include social, political, and environmental messages, making the Carnival an event where celebration intertwines with profound cultural expression.

Diwali

Diwali, also known as Deepavali, is one of the most important Hindu holidays, lasting five days. It represents the spiritual triumph of light over darkness, of good over evil, of knowledge over ignorance. Each Diwali day has its own set of customs and significance, which include worship, family gatherings, and festival activities. People decorate their houses and public spaces with oil lamps and colorful floor decorations during Diwali. Fireworks and firecrackers play an important role in the celebration. It is a time for families and friends to share gifts and sweets, and it's also a time for cleaning and rejuvenation of houses and more importantly, relationships.

Chinese New Year

Chinese New Year, also known as the Spring Festival, marks the start of the lunar new year and is based on the Chinese lunar calendar. The event begins with the new moon, which occurs between January 21 and February 20. Each year in the Chinese calendar is associated with one of the 12 Chinese zodiac animals, and the animal sign of the year is said to impact the qualities of the year and the individuals born in it. The Chinese New Year is marked by a variety of culturally significant customs and traditions. It is family reunion season, and many people travel vast distances to be with their loved ones. Traditional activities include the distribution of red envelopes, known as hongbao containing money, which is meant to bring good luck and prosperity. The festival is also marked by lion and dragon dances, fireworks, and special meals. Cleaning the house before the New Year is a common practice, symbolizing the sweeping away of bad fortune and making way for good incoming luck.

Holi

Holi, also known as the Festival of Colors, is celebrated by people smearing colored powder, spraying colored water, and throwing water balloons on each other. The use of colors symbolizes the arrival of spring and the victory of good over evil. The festival is characterized by scenes of people covered in bright, multicolored powders, creating a joyous and playful atmosphere. Holi has deep cultural and mythological roots. It's primarily associated with the legend of Holika and Prahlad in Hindu mythology, which demonstrates the triumph of faith and goodness over evil. Additionally, Holi is linked to the love story of Krishna and Radha, and in many regions, it's celebrated with traditional dances and songs that reflect this aspect. The festival promotes social harmony, where barriers of caste, creed, and age are set aside, and everyone joins in the fun and festivities. It's a time for forgiveness and new beginnings, fostering a spirit of togetherness and community.

THANK YOU FOR CHOOSING

OUR BOOK

BOOKS IN THIS SERIES

3 Books: Amazing Discoverers Series: Fun Facts for Kids, Teens & Adults

by

ANDY RYAN

- ➢ 108 Quirky Facts for Super Smart Kids
- ➢ 108 Fun Facts for Super Smart Kids
- ➢ 108 Amazing Facts for Super Smart Kids

NOTES